LEYLAND BUSES

SINCE 1955

STEWART J. BROWN

Ian Allan PUBLISHING

First published 2012

ISBN (13) 978 0 7110 3652 9

© Ian Allan Publishing Ltd 2012

Published by Ian Allan Publishing

an imprint of Ian Allan Publishing Ltd, Hersham, Surrey, KT12 4RG.
Printed in England by Ian Allan Printing Ltd, Hersham, Surrey, KT12 4RG.

Visit the Ian Allan Publishing website at www.ianallanpublishing.com

Front cover: The Scottish Bus Group embraced the PD3 Titan with enthusiasm, between 1957 and 1961 taking 325 PD3/3s, all with 67-seat lowbridge bodies, vacuum brakes and manual gearboxes. Western SMT was the biggest user, with 186. These were bodied by Northern Counties, Burlingham and, as seen here in Irvine in 1977, by Alexander. SBG companies also ran large numbers of PD2s, between them operating more than 350. *Stewart J. Brown collection*

Back cover: A contrast in Wigan in 1973. The one-man-operated Northern Counties-bodied Panther loading on the right is one of 12 delivered to Wigan Corporation in 1970 and is a dual-door 46-seater. The Titan pulling out behind it is a PD2A/27 with manual gearbox, new in 1962 and with 64-seat bodywork by Massey. Both Massey and Northern Counties were based in Wigan. *John Aldridge*

Previous page: A fine selection of BET-group Leylands in Buxton in the mid-1960s. The first three buses belong to Trent. Nearest the camera is a 1965 Leopard PSU3/1R with synchromesh gearbox and 49-seat Willowbrook body. Alongside is a Tiger Cub with 44-seat Weymann body, one of 60 buses delivered in two batches in 1956 and 1957. Next comes another 36ft Leopard. The coach at the far end is a North Western Leopard with Alexander Y-type body, *en route* to London. *John Aldridge*

CONTENTS

Above: In 1993 Alexander built a batch of 19 RH bodies on Cummins-engined Olympian chassis, and these were bought by four operators – United Automobile, Keighley & District, London Buslines and Sheffield Omnibus. The last-named had commenced operation in 1991 using ex-Preston Atlanteans (hence the Preston-style livery) and would be taken over by Yorkshire Traction in 1995. There were five of these Olympians in the Sheffield Omnibus fleet, and they were 74-seaters. *Stewart J. Brown*

INTRODUCTION

IN THE 1950s LEYLAND WAS a force to be reckoned with. There were Titans and Tigers in service from Inverness in the north to Plymouth in the south. Leyland was the main supplier of buses to most of the biggest municipal fleets, as well as to British Electric Traction and the Scottish Bus Group. The company was a major exporter too, and Leyland buses could be found in Australasia, much of Africa and parts of South America.

There was a self-assuredness about the company. The merger with Associated Commercial Vehicles in 1962 created an even more powerful business. Then, alas, it started to unravel. The turning-point was the creation, at the behest of the Government, of the British Leyland Motor Corporation. This united the successful Leyland commercial vehicle organisation with the struggling British Motor Holdings. The merged company had myriad competing products, particularly in its car ranges. It was facing growing foreign competition, notably from Japanese car makers and European truck builders. And it had to be bailed out by the Government in 1975.

Most of the investment in BLMC was being directed towards cars. Buses and coaches were, it seemed, at the bottom of the list. There was growing competition in the UK bus and coach market too, some of it from Europe, some of it from new UK-based manufacturers. Leyland's reaction was often simply too late. Between 1979 and 1987 there were major factory closures – AEC, Park Royal, Bristol, ECW and Roe. And bus-industry deregulation and privatisation in the mid-1980s saw demand for new big buses dwindle. Leyland's bus division was fatally weakened; after it was sold to its management and then quickly re-sold to Volvo, rationalisation was quick and inevitable. The Leyland name vanished from the bus business in 1993.

For those familiar with the company's great days in the 1950s or the 1960s, a world without Leyland was unimaginable. But it happened. The pages that follow feature the products of Britain's biggest bus manufacturer from its mid-1950s peak to the end of production.

Stewart J. Brown
Hebden Bridge
May 2012

3

A PROUD TRADITION

BY 1955, LEYLAND MOTORS HAD been building trucks and buses for almost 50 years. The company had adopted the Leyland name in 1907, having been created in 1896 as the Lancashire Steam Motor Co. It was Britain's biggest bus builder, and its products could be seen the length and breadth of Britain – and in many overseas markets too. It was a remarkable success story, and that success was based on buses (and trucks) which were soundly engineered and reliable in operation.

It's surprising to consider that in 1955 Leyland's UK bus range consisted of just two purpose-designed models – the Titan and the Tiger Cub. The Titan name had been adopted in 1927. The 1955 models were the 27ft-long PD2 which dated from 1947 and was powered by Leyland's 9.8-litre O.600 engine, and the mid-engined Tiger Cub which had the smaller 5.76-litre O.350 horizontal engine and had been introduced in 1952. The PD2 was joined by the 30ft-long PD3 in 1956.

The most innovative product in the company's history, the double-deck Atlantean, entered production in 1958 and set the standard for the future with its rear-mounted engine and set-back front axle, allowing the entrance to be located opposite the driver. The improvements being made to Britain's trunk roads, and the start of construction of a network of motorways, saw a growing demand for coaches designed for sustained high-speed long-distance running. Leyland met this demand with its O.600-engined Leopard,

introduced in 1959. This chassis, in various guises, was to enjoy a 22-year production life.

Pressure from the Scottish Bus Group saw the introduction in 1961 of a low-height equivalent of the Titan. The Lowlander was badged as an Albion in Scotland and as a Leyland in England. Its drop-centre rear axle was also offered as an option in the Atlantean, allowing Leyland to build a low-height model to compete with Daimler's increasingly popular Fleetline.

Against a backdrop of declining patronage, urban bus operators were looking for ways to cut costs in the 1960s and alighted on one-man-operated single-deckers as the way forward. To meet this demand Leyland introduced the rear-engined Panther (36ft long) and the Panther Cub (33ft long) in 1964. A small number of Panthers were bodied as coaches.

The Leyland organisation expanded dramatically in the 1960s. Leyland was the dominant partner in the 1962 merger with Associated Commercial Vehicles, which owned rival chassis manufacturer AEC and bodybuilders Park Royal and Roe. In 1965 Leyland acquired a stake in Bristol and Eastern Coach Works. And with Government intervention the Leyland Motor Corporation was merged with British Motor Holdings in 1968 to create the British Leyland Motor Corporation. BMH brought with it the Guy and Daimler bus businesses, along with many of Britain's best-known car marques – Austin, Austin-Healey, MG, Morris, Riley and Wolseley.

1955 Titan
At the end of 1955, Southend Corporation received the first of a batch of a dozen PD2/12s with exposed radiators, manual gearboxes and lowbridge Massey bodies. They were 55-seaters and would serve the town for 16 years. *Harry Hay*

5

Above: **1956 Titan**

One of Leyland's 1930s advertising campaigns ran, 'Buy a Titan and bury a tram.' The spirit of the message lived on in the 1950s when, from 1954-57, Edinburgh Corporation bought 300 Titans to replace its trams. These were PD2/20 models, with synchromesh gearboxes and vacuum brakes. They had lightweight Metro-Cammell Orion bodies – the complete 63-seat buses weighed just 6 tons 15 cwt unladen. *Stewart J. Brown*

Right: **1957 Titan**

Not surprisingly, the Leyland Titan was the preferred choice of double-decker for most Lancashire municipal fleets, as they supported their local bus manufacturer. Many also supported local bodybuilders, and this PD2/20 in the Lytham St Annes fleet was one of five 58-seaters delivered in 1957 with bodywork by Northern Counties of Wigan. It is heading from Blackpool to St Annes on a service operated jointly with Blackpool Corporation, which also ran Titans on the route – both fleets were at the time 100% Leyland. *John Aldridge*

1957 Tiger Cub

King Alfred Motor Services of Winchester was one of many small firms which bought Tiger Cubs in the 1950s, taking nine between 1953 and 1959, all bodied by Weymann. The two delivered in 1957 were dual-purpose 41-seaters. Passengers board in Winchester in April 1973, a few days before the King Alfred business was purchased by NBC's Hants & Dorset company. They were at that time the oldest buses in the King Alfred fleet and at 16 years of age were nearing the end of their lives. *Stewart J. Brown*

1959 Titan
A number of BET companies saw the benefits of running high-capacity 30ft-long Titans, and the two biggest users, Ribble and Southdown, opted for forward-entrance full-fronted bodies. Those for Southdown were built by Northern Counties, as seen on this 1959 69-seat PD3/4 in Brighton in 1971, freshly repainted in the company's traditional livery but with Southdown-BH&D fleetnames, after the amalgamation by the National Bus Company of Southdown with Brighton Hove & District but before the arrival of NBC's corporate leaf-green colours. Southdown built up a fleet of 285 PD3s – the UK's largest – between 1957 and 1967. *John Aldridge*

Above: **1960 Atlantean**

Wallasey Corporation was famously the first operator to put a production Atlantean into service, in November 1958. By mid-1960 there were 20 in the 90-strong fleet. Here one of the 1960 buses, with 76-seat Metro-Cammell body, leads two other municipal Leylands from north-west England – Titans from Widnes and St Helens. This strange mix of vehicles might look like a modern bus rally, but this is 1969, and the buses are operating special services around Caernarvon (as it was then spelt) for the investiture of the Prince of Wales. *John Aldridge*

Right: **1960 Titan**

The Titan was popular with operators large and small. This PD3/1 with 69-seat Northern Counties body was new to AA Motor Services of Ayr in 1960. The short bay in mid-wheelbase was a feature of most 30ft-long forward-entrance Northern Counties bodies. New Titans were at this time being bought by a number of Scottish independents. The last would be a PD2A for A1 of Ardrossan, in 1965. *Harry Hay*

Above: 1963 Titan
Leyland was the last manufacturer to build double-deck chassis suitable for 7ft 6in-wide bodywork, supplying small numbers in the 1960s. The availability of narrow Titans was one factor which led to Colchester Corporation abandoning AEC, which had stopped production of its 7ft 6in-wide Regent V, and taking delivery of Leylands for the first time in 1960. This PD2A/31 with 61-seat Massey body was one of seven which joined the fleet in 1963. The 'A' suffix in the chassis code indicated a vehicle fitted with the St Helens-style new-look bonnet and grille, introduced in 1961 to replace the previous new-look front, designed for Midland Red. *Stewart J. Brown*

Right: 1963 Titan
In the early 1960s Leeds City Transport shared its chassis orders between AEC, Daimler and Leyland. In 1963 Leyland supplied ten 30ft-long PD3A/2 Titans, with Pneumocyclic gearboxes and air brakes. They had 70-seat rear-entrance Weymann Orion bodies. By this time, however, the Titan was on the way out; 1963 was the first year in which sales of Atlantean outnumbered those of Titans. *Stewart J. Brown*

1963 Tiger Cub
The Tiger Cub was one of the standard models in the Alexander fleet from 1954. This coach was one of 31 with 41-seat Alexander Y-type bodywork delivered to Alexander Midland in 1963/4. In total, 282 Tiger Cubs were bought new by Alexander and by its post-1961 Fife and Midland successors. This coach is seen when new, awaiting custom outside the Midland tours office in Glasgow.
Stewart J. Brown

1963 Lowlander

Developed primarily for the Scottish Bus Group and badged as an Albion, the Lowlander was a low-height alternative to the PD3. It had the same O.600 engine, but with a remote-mounted gearbox and a drop-centre rear axle. Southend Corporation, which operated lowbridge PD3s, took 10 Lowlanders with Alexander bodies in 1963. This is a 1971 photograph, by which time the Lowlanders had been equipped for one-man operation. The sign mounted under the comprehensive destination display could be switched on to advise intending passengers that the bus was being operated without a conductor. Lowlander production totalled 274 vehicles, of which 193 went to SBG companies. *John Aldridge*

Above: 1965 Leopard

The original Leopards were coded L1 (bus) and L2 (coach) and were introduced in 1959. The Leopard used a horizontal version of the O.600 engine and was thus a more powerful alternative to the O.350-engined Tiger Cub. Late buyers of the L2 included the Samuelson New Transport Co, a BET-associated company which operated a fleet of 14 coaches in London. In 1965 it took four L2Ts – the 'T' indicating the optional two-speed rear axle – with 41-seat Harrington bodies. This one is seen on the Embankment in 1973, operating on hire to London Transport on a sightseeing tour. *Stewart J. Brown*

Right: 1965 Leopard

The most successful of the Leopards was the 36ft-long PSU3, widely used both as a service bus and as a touring coach. It was introduced in 1961 in response to that year's revision of the Construction & Use Regulations, which permitted buses and coaches to be 36ft long. The model was favoured by many BET companies, including Ribble, owner of this 1965 coach with Plaxton Panorama I body, seen leaving Glasgow on the X30 express service to Manchester. Ribble was a big user of the Leopard in the 1960s and took 83 in 1965 alone, a mixture of buses and coaches. *Harry Hay*

Above: **1965 Titan**

Most 1960s Titans had concealed radiators, but some operators preferred the traditional exposed radiator, primarily because it offered better access to the engine. These included Halifax, which in 1965 took delivery of eight PD2/37s with 65-seat Roe bodies. The very last UK Titan, ordered by Ramsbottom Urban District Council but delivered in November 1969 to the newly created SELNEC PTE, was an exposed-radiator PD3. *Stewart J. Brown*

1965 Atlantean

London Transport was at the start of the 1960s committed to the Routemaster and was slow to evaluate rear-engined double-deckers. The first were 50 Atlanteans and eight Daimler Fleetlines, delivered in 1965. They had Park Royal bodies, which on the Atlanteans were fitted with just 72 seats, at a time when 78 was the norm in a rear-engined double-decker. Originally crew-operated, they were later converted for one-man operation, as seen here in Croydon in January 1973. A few months later, all 50 Atlanteans were sold to China Motor Bus in Hong Kong. When LT placed bulk orders for rear-engined double-deckers it opted for the Fleetline rather than the Atlantean. *Stewart J. Brown*

1965 Atlantean

Just 31 Atlanteans were bodied by Massey of Wigan, the biggest user being Maidstone Corporation, which had 20. The only other buyers of Massey-bodied Atlanteans were Colchester Corporation and A1 Service of Ardrossan. Both Maidstone and Colchester had previously bought Massey-bodied Titans. This is a 1965 PDR1/1 Mk II in Maidstone, one of eight which were the operator's first rear-engined buses. The Mk II designation, which was not widely used, indicated various minor design modifications introduced in 1963. The destination is intriguing – was there only one building in Westmorland Road with a blue door? *Stewart J. Brown*

1967 Titan
The last front-engined buses for Leicester City Transport, delivered in 1967, were 20 PD3A/12s, the body order being divided equally between East Lancs (as seen here) and Metro-Cammell. All were 74-seaters. They brought to 117 the number of PD3s delivered to Leicester since 1958, the type making up just over half of the fleet's 210 buses. They were followed in 1968/9 by 20 Atlanteans, which would be Leicester's last Leyland double-deckers. From 1967 the 'A' chassis-code suffix indicated the fitting of a revised version of the Pneumocyclic gearbox, rather than the use of the St Helens-style bonnet. *Stewart J. Brown*

1968 Panther

Inspired by Continental European practice, Sunderland Corporation replaced half of its fleet between 1966 and 1968 with 90 new one-man-operated 36ft-long single-deckers with distinctively styled bodywork. Most of these new buses were Strachans-bodied Panthers. This is one of 24 delivered in 1968. The Panther used the horizontal O.600 engine and was launched in 1964. It was phased out in 1972, after almost 700 deliveries to British operators, and was replaced by the integral Leyland National. *Stewart J. Brown*

1968 Titan

It's a measure of the diversity in operating practices in the 1960s that buses as different as this exposed-radiator Titan and the Panther in the previous picture could both have entered service in the same year. The Panther exuded modernity; this Wigan Titan was the epitome of municipal conservatism. That the Titan was the better bus in terms of reliability is indisputable, but whatever the problems of the Panther, the concept of a rear-engined low-floor bus was the way forward. This handsome bus is a PD2/37 with 64-seat Massey body. The Titans delivered to Wigan in 1968 were its last, and were also the last exposed-radiator PD2s. The Wigan fleet was at this time 100% Leyland. *John Aldridge*

1968 Panther Cub
The Panther Cub was 33ft long and had Leyland's horizontal O.400 engine. It had a short life, being produced from 1964 to 1968. Total production was 94, including one demonstrator. The last Panther Cubs entered service with Brighton Corporation. There were seven – three with Strachans bodies, as seen here, and four bodied by Marshall. Before the Panther Cubs Brighton had been buying Titans. Subsequent purchases were Atlanteans. *Stewart J. Brown*

1968 Atlantean

An alternative to the Panther Cub was to fit single-deck bodywork to an Atlantean chassis. While single-deck Fleetlines were fairly common, single-deck Atlanteans were extremely rare, just 17 being built new. This is one of three that were supplied to Great Yarmouth Transport and had 39-seat Marshall bodies. The others went to Portsmouth (12) and Merseyside PTE, which received two that had been ordered by Birkenhead Corporation. *Stewart J. Brown*

1968 Leopard

Another, more conservative, urban single-deck option in the late 1960s was the ultra-reliable high-floor mid-engined Leopard. This was the choice of Stockport Corporation, which took five PSU4/1Rs in 1968. They had dual-door 43-seat bodies by East Lancs and joined a fleet dominated by double-deck Titans. It's tempting to enquire whether Councillor Lane was a place or a person ... *John Aldridge*

1968 Atlantean

The 33ft-long Atlantean PDR2/1 was introduced in 1967. The long-wheelbase chassis proved popular with a small number of urban fleets, most notably in Leeds, Manchester, Plymouth and Sheffield. For its long Atlanteans Sheffield standardised on dual-door Park Royal bodies. This 79-seater was one of 50 delivered in 1968/9. The long-wheelbase PDR2/1 was destined to have a short production life, being replaced in 1972 by the improved AN68/2. *Stewart J. Brown*

1968 Leopard

The expansion of the motorway network in the 1960s helped boost interest in heavy-duty coaches which could cover long distances with ease, and at this time there were two main choices – the Leyland Leopard and the AEC Reliance. Maidstone & District took 12 Leopard PSU3A/4s with Pneumocyclic gearboxes and Duple's recently restyled Commander III body in 1968. One pulls out of London's Victoria Coach Station in the summer of 1973. *Stewart J. Brown*

1968 Panther
Southport Corporation, which was running a fleet of Titans, switched to Panthers in 1968 when it placed in service 12 with 45-seat dual-door Metro-Cammell bodies, which featured deeper windows in the forward, low-floor section of the body. This one is seen in Lord Street in 1974, shortly after the Southport operation had been absorbed by Merseyside PTE. Ten more Panthers, but with Marshall bodies, arrived in 1971. *Stewart J. Brown*

1968 Atlantean

From 1964 Leyland offered a low-height Atlantean, with a drop-centre rear axle – first the PDR1/2 and then, from 1967, the PDR1/3. Six PDR1/3s entered service with East Midland in 1968 and had low-height Alexander bodies of a style more commonly associated with the Daimler Fleetline. This one, freshly repainted in NBC's corporate leaf-green livery, is seen leaving Doncaster's south bus station in 1973. The option of a low-height Atlantean disappeared when the PDR-series models were replaced by the AN68 in 1972; the new model was not offered with a drop-centre rear axle. The PDR1/3 was a rare model, just 81 being built. It was rendered redundant following the creation of BLMC and the subsequent availability of a Leyland engine in the Daimler Fleetline chassis.
Stewart J. Brown

1973 Atlantean

Glasgow Corporation was one of the early operators to standardise on the Atlantean, and by the summer of 1973, when its operations were acquired by Greater Glasgow PTE, was running almost 700, all bodied by Alexander. For a brief period dual-door bodywork was specified, as on this 1973 AN68, which was among the last new buses supplied to the Corporation but is seen in the city centre after being repainted in PTE colours. By the mid-1970s new Alexander-bodied AN68s were replacing early PDR1s in the Glasgow fleet. The Corporation and the PTE between them bought 1,449 new Atlanteans, the last entering service in 1981.
Stewart J. Brown

IMPROVED MODELS, NEW DIRECTIONS

THE BRITISH LEYLAND MOTOR CORPORATION inherited a multiplicity of competing models, and rationalisation was needed. The first sign of this was a milestone in Leyland's bus development: a joint venture with the National Bus Company to produce an integral single-decker, the Leyland National. It was highly standardised, using car-like production methods which largely eliminated the need to employ skilled tradesmen in its manufacture. That it didn't meet with universal acceptance was due to a number of factors, including its relative sophistication, its use of the new (and noisy) turbocharged 8.2-litre 500-series engine and its integral construction, which meant buyers had no choice of bodybuilder. In an industry used to bespoke vehicles, the National, introduced in 1972, was not an unqualified success.

Leyland also planned to rationalise its double-deck range by replacing the Atlantean, the Daimler Fleetline and the Bristol VRT with one integral model, known initially by its project code, B15. The first prototypes were trialled by London Transport in 1976. By the time the B15 entered series production as the Titan in 1978, Leyland had accepted that operators were still going to want to buy from bodybuilders such as Alexander and Northern Counties, and in 1980 it launched the real replacement for its three double-deck chassis – the Olympian. The last UK Atlanteans entered service in 1984. The Titan and the Olympian were the first Leyland bus models to offer the option of engines sourced from an outside supplier, Gardner; hitherto all Leyland buses had been offered exclusively with Leyland engines.

A front-engined bus chassis, derived from the Terrier light truck, was marketed as the Cub from 1979. Fewer than 40 were bought by mainstream bus operators. Production ended in 1986 when Leyland's Bathgate factory closed.

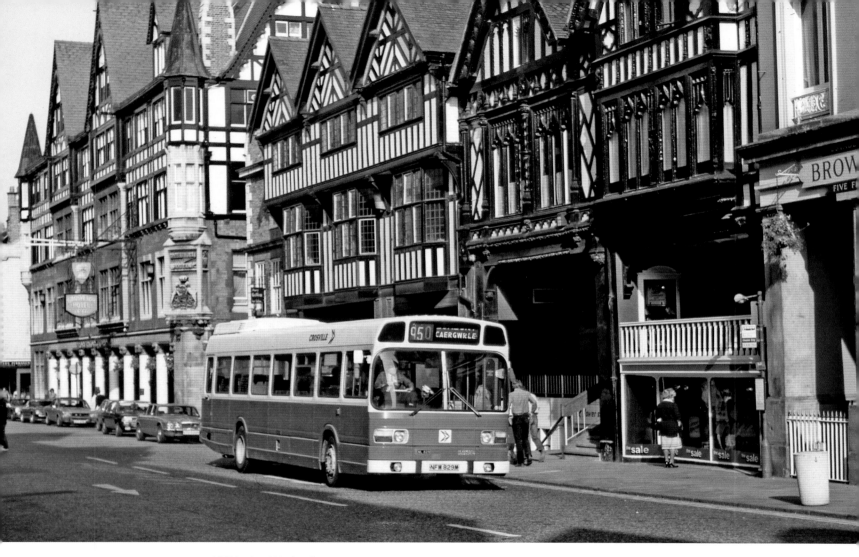

1973 Leyland National

When Leyland and NBC teamed up to produce an all-new integral bus it was clear that NBC would be a major customer. In the winter of 1973/4 Crosville took a batch of 46 Nationals which had 48 high-backed seats and were in NBC's local-coach livery, as seen here in Chester. They were 11.3m long. NBC would indeed prove to be the biggest user of the National, taking almost 4,800 over a period of 14 years, from a total production of around 7,500. *Stewart J. Brown*

Right: **1974 Atlantean**
Leeds City Transport had standardised on long-wheelbase Atlanteans and Fleetlines which were fitted with two-door Roe bodies with panoramic windows. But the last body of this style was a one-off delivered in the summer of 1974 to Colin S. Pegg of Caston, on an AN68/2 chassis. It was a 78-seater in an unusual pink livery. The figures in the chassis code denoted the use of the 680 engine, a development of the O.600, while the letters indicated AtlanteaN. *Stewart J. Brown*

Below: **1974 Atlantean**
During the period 1974-81 NBC bought 435 AN68 Atlanteans with bodies to this design, produced by both Park Royal and the associated Roe business. The biggest users were London Country, Ribble, Northern General and Southdown. Here a 1974 Park Royal-bodied bus of Southdown picks up passengers on the seafront at Brighton as it heads along the coast to Eastbourne. In total, NBC purchased 526 bodies of this style on Atlantean chassis, the first 90 being PDR1A/1 models for London Country in 1972, the last a one-off to rebody a damaged Yorkshire Woollen bus. *Stewart J. Brown*

1975 Leyland National
All seven PTEs operated Leyland Nationals. Six short dual-door Nationals were delivered to South Yorkshire in 1975 and were used initially on the Sheffield City Clipper service, which provided a link between various parts of the city centre. The 10.3m National had shorter side windows than the 11.3m model except in the bay immediately ahead of the rear axle, which was the same length on both models; this meant that on buses with a centre exit door there was a standard structure for the door area irrespective of the vehicle's length. *Stewart J. Brown*

1976 Leopard
The least-common Leopard was the shortest model, the PSU4, which replaced the L1 and L2 in 1965. Three PSU4C/2Rs were delivered to Chester City Transport at the start of 1976 and had 43-seat Northern Counties bodies. The PSU4 was nominally 10m long. *Stewart J. Brown*

1976 Leyland National
Unique in the UK was this 10.9m-long National built in 1973 as a prototype for an Australian specification. Up to the rear axle it had the long bays of the 11.3m model, while the last two side windows used the shorter bays of the 10.3m bus. Bought (and first registered) by Rennie of Dunfermline in 1976, it is seen here in Preston in 1982 in the ownership of Fishwick of Leyland, which was also a regular buyer of new Nationals. *Stewart J. Brown*

1976 Leyland National

London Transport was one of the biggest customers for the Leyland National, taking 437 of the original model, followed by 69 National 2s, to give a total of 506 bought new over an eight-year period from 1973 to 1981. Here a Westlink bus leaves Hounslow bus station in 1990. It came from a batch of 51 delivered in 1976. When Westlink was created as a London Buses subsidiary in 1986 its fleet comprised 28 Nationals. *Peter Rowlands*

1976 Leopard
The length limit for buses and coaches was increased in 1969, to 12m (39ft 4in), and Leyland developed a longer Leopard, the PSU5. A 12m coach could seat up to 57, compared with 49 in a typical 36ft model. The Leopard was supplied as a coach to most NBC companies in the 1970s, and this PSU5A/4R, with 51-seat Duple Dominant body, was one of 11 delivered to National Travel North West in 1976. It is seen in 1984, making a spirited exit from London's Park Lane on the service to Manchester. *Stewart J. Brown*

1976 Leopard
A more basic NBC Leopard coach was this PSU3C/4R operated by Eastern Counties and photographed in Ipswich in 1977.
One of a batch of seven with Alexander's new T-type body, it was a 49-seater. In total, NBC took 37 T-type Leopards, delivered
in 1976 and shared between six of its subsidiaries. *Stewart J. Brown*

1977 Atlantean

A number of independents bought Atlanteans in the 1970s, and in Scotland they generally specified Alexander bodywork. Two AN68/1Rs with panoramic-windowed Alexander bodies were bought by Graham's Bus Service of Paisley in 1977 and were followed by two more in 1979. *Stewart J. Brown*

1979 Leyland National

Some NBC companies wanted a simpler version of the National, and this appeared in 1978 as the B-series. It was available only as a 10.3m bus, and the most obvious difference was the adoption of a conventional heating system which eliminated the roof-mounted heating pod of the original model. It also used a de-rated version of the 500-series engine, with a power output of 150bhp instead of the 170bhp of the standard model, which now became the A-series. London Country was a big user of the B-series, and this bus, pausing in Epsom on the service from West Croydon to Guildford, was one of 168 delivered in 1978/9. They were 41-seaters. NBC and Leyland talked about the B-series National as a replacement for the Bristol LH, but it was clearly a very different type of vehicle from the straightforward low-cost Bristol. *Stewart J. Brown*

1979 Atlantean

A batch of 52 Alexander-bodied Atlanteans was delivered to the South Yorkshire PTE in 1979/80, and at the PTE's insistence
these had Voith gearboxes rather than the standard Pneumocyclic. They were dual-door 74-seaters. Although in the 1970s Leyland
introduced revised codes for what seemed like quite minor chassis modifications, the Voith-fitted Atlanteans were simply AN68A/1Rs.
The Voith option was not promoted by Leyland, which no doubt was anxious to protect its own gearbox manufacturing, and no Voith
Atlanteans were supplied to any other operators. A benefit of the Voith transmission in hilly Sheffield was that it incorporated a
retarder. *Stewart J. Brown*

1980 Leopard

The Leopard's greatest success was with the Scottish Bus Group. Between 1960 and 1982 SBG bought 1,760 new Leopards, most with Alexander Y-type bodies. The Y-type buses, like this 1980 Midland Scottish vehicle in Glasgow, were licensed to carry 77 passengers – 53 seated and 24 standing. SBG's conservatism meant that most of its Leopards were PSU3/3Rs with manual gearboxes, although later deliveries, including this bus, were Pneumocyclic PSU3/4Rs. *Stewart J. Brown*

1980 DAB
The Workington factory, where the Leyland National was built, was intended to produce 2,000 buses a year but at best achieved around half that number. Various projects were developed to create more work, with differing degrees of success. One was the construction of bodywork on articulated chassis produced by Leyland's Danish associate, DAB, five being supplied to South Yorkshire PTE in 1980 for the Cityliner service in central Sheffield. The use of articulated buses lasted less than two years because of disputes over drivers' wage rates, and Leyland was soon seeking new homes for the buses. One was trialled by Aspden's of Blackburn on a school contract in March 1982. Similar National-bodied articulated DABs were bought by British Airways. *Stewart J. Brown*

Above: 1980 Atlantean
The long-wheelbase AN68/2 Atlantean, designed for bodywork around 33ft in length, was bought by a small number of urban operators, among them Tyne & Wear PTE. This was one of a batch of 50, with 86-seat Alexander bodywork, delivered in 1980. Other major AN68/2 users included the Blackpool and Preston municipal fleets. *Stewart J. Brown*

Right: 1980 Leyland National 2
The National 2 was launched in 1979, the principal change being the replacement of the unpopular 510 engine with the proven 680, as used in the Leopard. To accommodate the larger engine the radiator had to be moved from the rear of the bus to the front, increasing overall length by 300mm and requiring a new windscreen, which was of a design used by DAB. This is an early National 2 in the Cumberland fleet, seen in Workington bus station, just a few miles from the factory where the bus was built. The B-series model disappeared when the National 2 was introduced, but the absence of a roof pod reveals that Cumberland chose conventional under-seat heaters for this vehicle, an 11.6m 52-seater. *Stewart J. Brown*

1980 Atlantean

West Yorkshire PTE's typical bus from 1974 until the early 1980s was the Atlantean AN68/1R with this neat style of Roe bodywork. The bus on the left, new in 1980, shows the raised driving position that was standard on later Atlanteans. The difference is readily apparent when it is compared with the 1977 bus alongside in this 1986 view in central Bradford. *Stewart J. Brown*

1981 Leyland National 2
The Scottish Bus Group was a late convert to the Leyland National and after buying 68 of the original model in 1977/8 ordered batches of the Mk 2 version, taking 127 in 1980/1. These included ten 11.6m-long 52-seaters with 680 engines and Pneumocyclic gearboxes for Central SMT, delivered in 1981. One sign of the inflexibility of the National factory was its reluctance to apply complex liveries, and most SBG Nationals were delivered in one all-over colour – as on this bus in Balloch – to which cream relief was later added. *Stewart J. Brown*

1981 Atlantean

As well as taking Atlanteans with Park Royal and Roe bodies, NBC took smaller numbers with ECW bodies. A total of 188 AN68s were bodied by ECW for NBC between 1975 and 1981, and Ribble, with 82, was the biggest user. Among the last were 30 delivered in the winter of 1980/1. This one is seen in Southport bus station in 1986, shortly after Ribble's operations in Merseyside had been taken over by the newly created North Western company, in preparation for the privatisation of NBC. *Stewart J. Brown*

1981 Leopard

In the 1970s and early 1980s the Leopard was the coach of choice for many independent operators. Among these was Wallace Arnold of Leeds, one of the country's biggest coach operators, whose 1981 intake of new vehicles included 35 Leopards with Plaxton Supreme IV bodies. These were a mixture of 11m PSU3s and, as seen here in London, 12m PSU5s; all had Pneumocyclic gearboxes. This one displays the fleetname of Evan Evans, a London-based coach operator which was a Wallace Arnold subsidiary. It is pictured in Russell Square, with the imposing façade of the 1898 Hotel Russell as a backdrop. During the 1970s Wallace Arnold had bought on average 30 Leopards a year, but those delivered in 1981, along with three Tigers, were the company's last Leylands; most subsequent new coaches would be supplied by Volvo as the Swedish builder strengthened its presence in the coach market at Leyland's expense.
Stewart J. Brown

1981 Cub

To cater for a perceived demand for an inexpensive midibus Leyland developed the Cub. This was a modified Terrier truck chassis which featured a set-back front axle to accommodate an entrance opposite the driver. One of the few significant orders came from Lothian Region Transport, which bought 18 in 1981 for operation on lightly used services in Edinburgh. They had scaled-down Duple Dominant bus bodies with 31 seats. The only other big user of Cubs was West Yorkshire PTE, which took 15 with Optare bodies in 1986. The Cub was powered by a 5.65-litre Leyland 6.98NV engine. It was built at the Bathgate truck plant, and production ended when the factory closed in 1986. *Stewart J. Brown*

1981 Atlantean

One of the biggest buyers of AN68 Atlanteans was Greater Manchester PTE, which received 1,225, this figure including buses delivered to its predecessor SELNEC in the years 1972-4. By the time the last were delivered, in 1984, AN68 Atlanteans made up half of the fleet. This AN68 has a 75-seat Northern Counties body built to the PTE's standard design; a broadly similar body was built for the PTE by Park Royal. The bus behind is a Metrobus, produced by MCW, one of the late-1970s challengers to Leyland's dominance in the double-deck bus market. *Stewart J. Brown*

1982 Titan

The Titan was conceived by Leyland as a double-deck equivalent of the National – a complete integral vehicle to be built by Park Royal, with a limited choice of options. It was designed with the needs of London Transport very much in mind and had hydraulic brakes (at a time when air brakes were the preferred choice of most bus operators), independent front suspension and a new hydraulically actuated gearbox – the Hydracyclic – which incorporated a retarder. Production started at Park Royal in 1978 but was transferred to the under-utilised Workington plant when the Park Royal factory closed in 1980. LT ultimately took 1,125 of the 1,164 built. This is a 1982 example with, like most London Titans, a Gardner 6LXB engine; running as a crew-operated bus, it was photographed in 1984 heading west along the Strand. *Stewart J. Brown*

1982 Olympian

Like most major bus manufacturers Leyland traditionally ran demonstrators which it would sell after two or three years' use. However, the practice changed in the 1970s when the Government began subsidising the purchase of new buses; New Bus Grant typically covered 50% of the purchase price but was available only to bus operators, not to manufacturers. Consequently Leyland started using operator-owned buses as demonstrators, among them this 1982 Gardner-engined Olympian from the West Yorkshire PTE fleet. Fitted with a 76-seat Roe body, it is seen operating on loan to Alexander Fife. Early Olympians like this one were built at Bristol; production was transferred to Workington in 1983 when the Bristol factory was closed. *Stewart J. Brown*

Leyland

A GIANT IN DECLINE

BY 1980 THE LEOPARD WAS looking distinctly out of date, and independent coach operators were increasingly buying imported chassis, primarily from Volvo (from 1972) and DAF (from 1975). Leyland's belated response was the mid-engined Tiger, launched in 1981. At the start of the 1980s there was also growing interest in rear-engined integral coaches. For this market Leyland developed the integral Royal Tiger Doyen. A Royal Tiger underframe was also made available, and small numbers were bodied by Plaxton and Van Hool.

Volvo had in 1982 introduced Britain's first – and only – successful underfloor-engined double-deck chassis, the Citybus. In 1986 Leyland responded with the Lion, based on an underframe from the group's Danish associate, DAB. Volvo sold 586 Citybuses; Leyland sold just 32 Lions. At the same time Leyland turned to DAB for a midibus, the Tiger Cub, to be imported part-built and then trimmed at ECW. Only two were built.

The National had been updated in 1979 with a bigger engine, the 680, to replace the original 510 (both figures indicating the engine's size in cubic inches). A Gardner option was added in 1982. Unusual applications of the National structure included rail vehicles, as well as bodywork for a small number of DAB-based articulated buses. In 1985 the National was replaced by a new city bus, the Lynx, with a choice of Leyland or Gardner engines. For the UK it was sold as a complete bus, but Leyland's aim, never fulfilled, was to develop links with overseas bodybuilders to assemble bodies on Lynx underframes for export markets.

The Tiger was offered with a Gardner engine from 1984, but with demand for both Gardner and Leyland engines declining, both Leyland Bus and Leyland Trucks started using Cummins power. The Cummins L10 was offered in the Olympian (from 1985), Tiger (1986) and Lynx (1987). The Leyland Hydracyclic gearbox was also dropped, replaced by a ZF automatic.

The last new bus model from Leyland, in 1987, was the Swift. This was intended to be a low-cost bus for the newly deregulated industry and had a vertical Cummins engine mounted under the floor. It had limited success as a bus but was, briefly, moderately popular as a coach.

BLMC had been rescued from collapse by the Government in 1975, becoming in effect a state-owned business. The Leyland Bus business was bought by its management in 1987 and then sold the following year to Volvo. Volvo quickly axed the Royal Tiger Doyen and the Swift. It re-engineered the Lynx and the Tiger to accept the 9.6-litre Volvo engine from 1990, although few Volvo-powered examples of either model were built. The last British Tigers entered service in 1991, while the last in the UK, for Northern Ireland, were delivered at the end of 1992. Lynx production ended in 1992. The one model which was of real value to Volvo was the Olympian, and that too was adapted to take a Volvo engine, being rebranded as a Volvo. The last UK Leyland Olympians entered service in 1993, but sales of Volvo Olympians would continue until 2000, when the move to low-floor buses brought production to an end.

1982 Leopard
The 12m-long PSU5 Leopard was typically fitted with high-quality coach bodywork. The ECW coach body produced for NBC in 1981/2 was not the most attractive of designs and, unlike most coach bodies of the time, didn't even merit a name, being known only by its Leyland development code, B51. The body was an update of that fitted to Bristol RELHs in the early 1970s, with shallower side windows and a new windscreen. Unfortunately the updating did not take account of the structural changes needed to fit the body to a mid-engined chassis, and the rear end of the B51 required strengthening after a short time in service. This is one of seven 53-seaters delivered to Hants & Dorset at the end of 1982 and is seen in London in the livery of the company's Shamrock & Rambler coaching operation. *Stewart J. Brown*

1983 Tiger

By the start of the 1980s the Leopard was being outclassed by coaches from mainland Europe and in particular by the Volvo B10M. Leyland's answer was the Tiger, which featured air suspension, a turbocharged TL11H engine and a front-mounted radiator. It was launched in 1981 and offered with either a ZF manual or a Pneumocyclic gearbox, the latter soon being replaced by the Hydracyclic. Whilst the model was intended to appeal to small coach operators, the biggest Tiger buyers were the state-owned NBC and SBG fleets. London Country bought Tigers for Green Line services, represented here by a 1983 Duple Dominant IV-bodied coach in London *en route* for Aylesbury. There were 45 vehicles in the batch. *Stewart J. Brown*

1983 Tiger

Even by the standards of the 1980s this West Riding Tiger was far from being a luxurious coach. It was one of a batch of five, and surely sits among the most unlikely vehicles ever to wear National Express livery. The 49-seat body was by Alexander, to the builder's TE specification, the 'E' standing for Express. Similar vehicles were delivered to other NBC subsidiaries, including Cumberland, East Midland and Eastern National, in 1983/4. *Stewart J. Brown*

1983 Titan

The only municipal buyer of new Titans was Reading Transport, which took 12. Ten of these were delivered in 1983. Five were fitted with Gardner 6LXCT engines and had single-door bodywork with 66 coach seats for operation on an express service to London. One is seen on the approach to Trafalgar Square. The other five 1983 vehicles had Gardner 6LXB engines, as fitted to the majority of Titans, and were of dual-door layout, with 70 seats. These – plus a demonstrator which yielded not a single order – were the only Workington-built Titans for an operator other than London Transport. *Stewart J. Brown*

1983 Olympian

Even before the Titan was launched, Leyland was aware that the model would not be acceptable to all operators. Apart from the lack of choice on the body, there was no low-height option, which was important to NBC and SBG. Thus was born the Olympian, initially with a choice of Leyland or Gardner engines. The standard NBC Olympian had a Gardner engine and low-height ECW bodywork which was clearly related to the Titan. This is a 1983 bus with 77-seat ECW body in the United Automobile fleet. The Olympian replaced the Atlantean, the Bristol VRT, the Daimler Fleetline and, ultimately, the integral Titan too. *Stewart J. Brown*

1983 Olympian

The long-wheelbase Olympian was a minority model in terms of UK sales. A number were supplied to NBC for use as coaches and had Leyland TL11 rather than Gardner engines. Maidstone & District used them on London services, and similar coaches were supplied to Alder Valley, Eastern National and London Country. The two-axle Olympian was essentially a commuter coach for NBC; for long-distance coaching NBC bought three-axle MCW Metroliners. The body was by ECW and had 73 coach seats.
Stewart J. Brown

1983 Olympian
The main UK buyer of long-wheelbase Olympians was Lothian Region Transport. The early vehicles had Leyland engines; later buses were Cummins-powered, an option offered when it was becoming clear that there was no long-term future for Leyland engine production. The first four batches comprised ONTL11/2R models with 81- or 83-seat dual-door bodywork by ECW. Subsequent vehicles – and two earlier trial buses – had Alexander bodies. When the Olympian metamorphosed into a Volvo, Lothian continued buying the type. Over 16 years Lothian took 297 Leyland Olympians followed by 134 built by Volvo. *Stewart J. Brown*

1983 Royal Tiger Doyen

A change was taking place in the coach business at the start of the 1980s with a growing interest in rear-engined integrals, led by Dutch manufacturer Bova and Germany's MAN. Leyland responded in 1982 with the Royal Tiger Doyen, initially built at the Roe factory in Leeds, and then from 1985 at the National factory in Workington, following the closure of Roe. It initially had a TL11H engine, as used in the Tiger, and the same choice of ZF manual or Leyland Hydracyclic gearboxes. Quality and production problems with early vehicles meant that the Doyen got off to a slow start, from which it never really recovered. This Roe-built coach for Hellyers of Fareham is seen at an exhibition organised by *Commercial Motor* magazine at Syon Park in 1983. Total Royal Tiger Doyen production amounted to barely 100, the model being dropped at the start of 1988 following Volvo's takeover of Leyland Bus.
Stewart J. Brown

Right: **1983 Tiger**

For 1983 Duple introduced two new body styles, the high-floor Caribbean and low-floor Laser replacing the ageing Dominant range and providing a more attractive match for the Tiger chassis. This Caribbean, in London's Victoria Coach Station, was one of five delivered to South Wales Transport in 1983. *Stewart J. Brown*

Below: **1984 Tiger**

Whereas most coach manufacturers seek commonality of style and parts between low- and high-floor coach bodies, Duple flew in the face of convention with the 3.5m-high Caribbean and 3.2m Laser, which were quite different designs. A total of 25 Duple-bodied Tigers delivered to National Welsh in 1984 comprised six Caribbeans and 19 Lasers, one of the latter being pictured here at the Minehead station of the West Somerset Railway. *Stewart J. Brown*

1984 Tiger
A number of Tigers were built as buses, among them nine for NBC's Midland Red North subsidiary in 1984. They had 51-seat Duple Dominant bodywork. This one is seen a few months after delivery, displaying the 'Hotspur' local identity used for services in the Shrewsbury area. *Stewart J. Brown*

1984 Royal Tiger
Having tried with the National and Titan to convince bus operators that integral construction was the future, Leyland did not make the same mistake with its integral coach and from the outset offered the Royal Tiger underframe to other bodybuilders. Only two – Plaxton and Van Hool – showed any interest. Travellers International of Hounslow took five Van Hool-bodied Royal Tigers in 1984 and another three in 1987, of just 25 bodied by the Belgian coachbuilder. Travellers also ran a large fleet of Van Hool-bodied Tigers. *Stewart J. Brown*

1984 Atlantean

The last home-market Atlanteans entered service in 1984, and the year's biggest delivery was to Merseyside PTE, which received 55 buses with 75-seat Alexander bodies. Here a brand-new AN68 approaches Liverpool's Pier Head. The five-bay body with its peaked domes, which had been specified by the PTE since 1972, looked distinctly old-fashioned by 1984. *Stewart J. Brown*

1984 Tiger

Under pressure from the Scottish Bus Group and fearful of losing business to Dennis, Leyland re-worked the Tiger chassis to accept a Gardner engine – a major job which required changes to the frame. Western Scottish was running Gardner-engined Seddon Pennines and Dennis Dorchesters, and in 1984 it took 20 Gardner-engined Tigers. These had 49-seat Plaxton Paramount 3200 bodies finished in Scottish Citylink livery. Most passed to the new Clydeside Scottish company in 1985, formed to take over the northern part of Western's business. This coach in Clydeside ownership is seen in Glasgow in 1986. *Stewart J. Brown*

1984 DAB

A bid to produce a midibus to act as a replacement for NBC's ageing Bristol LHs resulted in this vehicle, marketed as the Tiger Cub. It was a DAB integral, and Leyland's plan was to import built-up frames which would be trimmed and glazed at ECW. Only two were imported – this demonstrator and a vehicle that was operated by NBC's United Automobile subsidiary. *Stewart J. Brown*

1985 Lynx

National sales plummeted in the early part of the 1980s to the point where production was no longer viable, even with diversification into rail vehicles based on the National body. The National's replacement used a more conventional structure and was called the Lynx. Only one was supplied to NBC, being delivered to Ribble in 1985. Initially the Lynx was offered with the choice of Gardner or Leyland engines and a Hydracyclic gearbox. Later the standard drivetrain would be the Cummins/ZF combination.
Stewart J. Brown

1985 B21

The B21 was an export chassis which used the Leyland National's running gear and was an attempt to secure orders from markets which would not buy complete Nationals. A number went to Australia, and 10 were sold in the UK; six were tried by Ulsterbus as a possible successor to the Bristol RE, while four chassis from a cancelled export order were sold at a knockdown price to Ipswich Borough Transport. They had 690 engines and dual-door Alexander (Belfast) bodies. The B21 was built in Bristol, and the Ipswich buses carried Bristol badges. In total, fewer than 100 B21s were built. *Peter Rowlands*

1986 Olympian

All of the British builders of double-deck bodies (except MCW, which was concentrating on its integral Metrobus) built bodies for the Olympian. Northern Counties was the supplier of bodies on Olympians for Greater Manchester PTE and its successor, GM Buses. Deliveries in 1986 included 38 coach-seated vehicles for limited-stop services. Before the Olympian, Greater Manchester had bought both Fleetlines (with Gardner engines) and Atlanteans. It had 306 Olympians, of which just 16 were Leyland-engined, the rest being Gardner-powered. The chassis of this bus was built at Leyland's Farington plant, which in 1986 had taken over production from Workington. *Stewart J. Brown*

71

1986 Olympian

One of the biggest single UK orders for the Olympian came from London, once Leyland had decided to end Titan production. The order was for 260 with dual-door ECW bodies, and they were delivered in 1986/7. All had Gardner engines and Hydracyclic gearboxes. They were the last buses built by ECW, although bodywork of this style would be produced at Workington after ECW closed. *Stewart J. Brown*

Above: **1987 Lynx**
Merthyr Tydfil Transport took 12 Lynx 51-seaters in 1987, a bold investment in a future that was not to be. Under sustained competition the council-owned company closed in 1989, and the Lynxes were sold. The Merthyr Tydfil Lynxes had TL11H engines – an option dropped in 1988 when production of the engine ended.
Stewart J. Brown

Left: **1987 Lion**
Leyland Lion production totalled just 32 vehicles. The biggest user, with 19, was the Scottish Bus Group, and all of its Lions had Alexander R-type bodies. Six which had been built for Kelvin Scottish in 1986 were delivered in 1987 to Clydeside, where they were painted in the Quicksilver livery used for express services. One is seen leaving Glasgow's Buchanan bus station. The other 13 were operated by Eastern.
Stewart J. Brown

Above: 1989 Olympian

Stagecoach raised a few eyebrows in 1989 when it placed in service three Olympians with three axles – the first new tri-axle motor buses built for service in the UK for some 50 years. They had Alexander RL-type bodies, and two, fitted with 96 high-backed seats, were allocated to the Cumberland fleet. This one, with prominent Gardner badge on the front, is seen in Barrow-in-Furness. The tri-axle Olympians had 230bhp Gardner 6LXCT engines and cost around £110,000 each. *Stewart J. Brown*

Right: 1991 Olympian

This Cummins-engined Olympian had 76-seat bodywork built by Leyland at its Workington factory. The body was essentially that which had previously been built by Roe but with some detail differences. Between 1988 and 1992 Workington bodied 197 Olympians. Capital Citybus took 23 for operation on contracted services in London; this one was photographed loading at Wood Green in 1992. By now Olympian chassis production was back at Workington, following the closure earlier in the year of the Farington factory, which brought to an end the production of Leyland buses in the town from which they took their name. *Stewart J. Brown*

1991 Swift

Leyland's last new model was the high-floor Swift midibus, launched in 1987. This was available with a choice of two wheelbases, for vehicles with a nominal length of around 7m and 8m. It had a vertical 5.9-litre Cummins B-series engine located behind the front axle, and the choice of a Turner five-speed manual gearbox or an Allison AT545 automatic. Most Swifts were bodied by Wadham Stringer or Reeve Burgess. Two long-wheelbase Swifts with 39-seat Reeve Burgess Harrier bodies were supplied to Pennine Motor Services of Gargrave in the spring of 1991. They were the last new Swifts for a bus or coach operator, although a few later examples were supplied to local-authority welfare fleets. *Stewart J. Brown*

1992 Olympian
Stagecoach was a major Olympian user, initially with long-wheelbase models and then with standard-length 9.6m buses. In 1992 a batch of 25 with Gardner engines and Alexander RL bodies joined the group's Fife fleet. One is seen when new, leaving Edinburgh for Perth. *Stewart J. Brown*

Right: **1992 Lynx II**
The Lynx II was produced from 1990 to 1992 and had a revised front end to accommodate the intercooler for the Volvo engine which was an option on the new model. This bus was built as a Volvo demonstrator in 1992 and was purchased by Felix of Ilkeston, in whose ownership it is seen here in Derby bus station. Total Lynx production amounted to just over 1,000 vehicles.
Stewart J. Brown

Left: **1993 Olympian**
The last big order for Olympians in the UK was for 52 for Strathclyde Buses, which entered service in the latter half of 1993. They had Cummins L10 engines and 78-seat low-height Alexander bodies. Here the last of the batch passes through central Glasgow on its way to East Kilbride in the spring of 1994 when just a few months old. *Stewart J. Brown*

77

APPENDICES

1. THE TITAN CODE

Can't tell your PD2/1s from your PD2A/27s? Here's the key to the code. All models were powered by Leyland's O.600 engine.

Model	Wheelbase	Width	Transmission	Brakes	Grille	Notes
PD2/1	16ft 3in	7ft 6in	Manual	Vacuum		
PD2/3	16ft 3in	8ft	Manual	Vacuum		
PD2/4	16ft 3in	8ft	Manual	Air		
PD2/5	16ft 3in	8ft	Manual	Air		Blackpool
PD2/9	16ft 5in	7ft 6in	Manual	Vacuum		St Helens
PD2/10	16ft 5in	7ft 6in	Manual	Vacuum		
PD2/11	16ft 5in	7ft 6in	Pneumocyclic	Air		Leeds
PD2/12	16ft 5in	8ft	Manual	Vacuum		
PD2/13	16ft 5in	8ft	Manual	Air		
PD2/14	16ft 5in	8ft	Preselector	Air		Leeds
PD2/15	16ft 5in	8ft	Pneumocyclic	Air		Prototype
PD2/20	16ft 5in	8ft	Manual	Vacuum	BMMO	
PD2/21	16ft 5in	8ft	Manual	Air	BMMO	
PD2/22	16ft 5in	7ft 6in	Manual	Vacuum	BMMO	
PD2/23	16ft 5in	7ft 6in	Manual	Air	BMMO	
PD2/24	16ft 5in	8ft	Pneumocyclic	Air	BMMO	
PD2A/24	16ft 5in	8ft	Pneumocyclic	Air		St Helens
PD2/25	16ft 5in	7ft 6in	Pneumocyclic	Air	BMMO	
PD2A/25	16ft 5in	7ft 6in	Pneumocyclic	Air		St Helens
PD2/26	16ft 5in	8ft	Pneumocyclic	Air	BMMO	Lightweight
PD2/27	16ft 5in	7ft 6in	Manual	Air	BMMO	Lightweight
PD2A/27	16ft 5in	7ft 6in	Manual	Air		St Helens
PD2/28	16ft 5in	7ft 6in	Manual	Air	BMMO	
PD2A/28	16ft 5in	7ft 6in	Manual	Air		St Helens
PD2/30	16ft 5in	8ft	Manual	Vacuum	BMMO	
PD2A/30	16ft 5in	8ft	Manual	Vacuum		St Helens
PD2/31	16ft 5in	7ft 6in	Manual	Vacuum	BMMO	
PD2A/31	16ft 5in	7ft 6in	Manual	Vacuum		St Helens
PD2/34	16ft 5in	8ft	Pneumocyclic	Air		Manchester
PD2/35	16ft 5in	7ft 6in	Pneumocyclic	Air		
PD2/37	16ft 5in	8ft	Manual	Air		
PD2/38	16ft 5in	7ft 6in	Manual	Air		
PD2/40	16ft 5in	8ft	Manual	Vacuum		
PD2/41	16ft 5in	7ft 6in	Manual	Vacuum		
PD2A/44	16ft 5in	8ft	Pneumocyclic	Air		St Helens
PD2/47	16ft 5in	8ft	Manual	Air		St Helens
PD2A/54	16ft 5in	8ft	Pneumocyclic	Air		
PD2/57	16ft 5in	8ft	Manual	Air		
PD3/1	18ft 6in	8ft	Manual	Air	BMMO	
PD3A/1	18ft 6in	8ft	Manual	Air		St Helens
PD3/2	18ft 6in	8ft	Pneumocyclic	Air	BMMO	
PD3A/2	18ft 6in	8ft	Pneumocyclic	Air		St Helens
PD3/3	18ft 6in	8ft	Manual	Vacuum	BMMO	
PD3A/3	18ft 6in	8ft	Manual	Vacuum		St Helens
PD3/4	18ft 6in	8ft	Manual	Air		
PD3/5	18ft 6in	8ft	Pneumocyclic	Air		
PD3/6	18ft 6in	8ft	Manual	Vacuum		
PD3/11	18ft 6in	8ft	Manual	Air		St Helens
PD3A/12	18ft 6in	8ft	Pneumocyclic	Air		St Helens
PD3/14	18ft 6in	8ft	Manual	Air		
PD3A/15	18ft 6in	8ft	Pneumocyclic	Air		

The PD2/40 was the conservative model, with exposed radiator, manual gearbox and vacuum brakes. Ashton-under-Lyne Corporation took 24 with 65-seat rear-entrance Roe bodies between 1960 and 1964. *John Aldridge*

2. LEYLAND POWER

A quick guide to engines fitted.

Model	O.350/O.400	O.600	680	TL11	500-series	Gardner	Cummins L10	Volvo
Titan		x						
Tiger Cub	x							
Atlantean		x	x					
Leopard		x	x					
Lowlander		x						
Panther		x						
Panther Cub	x							
Royal Tiger Cub		x						
National					x			
Titan				x	x	x		
National 2			x	x		x		
Olympian				x		x	x	x
Tiger				x		x	x	x
Royal Tiger				x			x	
Lion				x				
Lynx				x		x	x	x

The Cub used a Leyland 6.98 engine, the Swift a Cummins B-series.